THE GIRAFFE IN THE GARDEN

By
Darshna Morzaria

AuthorHouse™ UK
1663 Liberty Drive
Bloomington, IN 47403 USA
www.authorhouse.co.uk
Phone: 0800.197.4150

Published by AuthorHouse 08/23/2018

ISBN: 978-1-5462-8768-1 (sc)
ISBN: 978-1-5462-8769-8 (e)

Print information available on the last page.

authorHOUSE®

About the

AUTHOR

Darshna Morzaria is a manager of her home-based nursery, Little Darling Childcare, in Harrow, west London. Although working from home, the children in her care enjoy the facilities resembling a nursery. This gives parents the confidence that their child is receiving the best of both types of early education – homely and professional.

Little Darling Childcare have incorporated the Forest School ethos into their setting. This is a great illustration of the passion to keep evolving and improving the skills and qualifications of all teachers so that they can offer every child the very best start in life.

In 2016, the nursery were shortlisted as a finalist in the coveted Nursery World Awards. In 2018, they achieved a Silver in the internationally-renowned RoSPA Health and Safety Awards.

This is the second published children's book by Darshna following her first, highly acclaimed, "The Big Yummy Treasure Chest".

Website: LittleDarling.co.uk
Twitter: @LittleDarlingHa
FaceBook: Facebook.com/LittleDarlingHarrow
YouTube: YouTube.com/c/LittleDarlingUK

But Sammy hated all exercise,

"I'm no good at sports, I'll never win a prize."

Sammy didn't know that
he needn't always win

That just being active
could leave him with a grin

Mum called on Darshna, in her they would confide,
"I'll get Sammy active, he'll love what I've outside!"

So off they went to Darshna's, she'd surely make him move,
He'd have great fun and learn a lot and see his health improve.

When they reached the house, they heard children laugh and play. But Sammy didn't know what he was going to meet that day.

There it was, a giraffe so tall,

Stood proud in the garden, a rare sight for all.

WOW, thought Sammy, he looks so sublime,
"Please say Darshna, I'm allowed to climb?"

"His name is George, try and reach his head",

So up clambered Sammy as he felt a little dread.

"Please let George and me go for a ride?"

"Of course," said Darshna, "take a tour outside."

Sammy held on tight as they strolled down the path,
Never did he think that he'd be riding a giraffe!

They couldn't go much further as they'd met a little stream,
But Sammy wasn't ready yet to give up on this dream.

"You know what, George, I will jump across the rocks",

"I'll climb down your neck, then take off my shoes and socks."

So off leapt Sammy, not giving George a chance

Once at the other side, he then did a victory dance.

Little Sammy loved watching TV' For hours
and hours it would fill him with glee.

"I worry about Sammy," said Dad to Mum.

"He spends so much time just sitting on his bum."

The time had come to go home, Sammy heard Mum and Dad,
"Thank you, George, for so much fun, the best I've ever had!"

Sammy smiled with glee, as they all walkaed down the drive,
"I think I'm going to run back home, I feel so alive!"

Printed in the United States
By Bookmasters